Genre Drama

MW00570688

Essential Question
What can you discover when you give
things a second look?

THE MYSTERIOUS TEACHER

by Feana Tu'akoi
illustrated by Andrew Burdan

Act 1
WHAT'S UP WITH MR. LIM?

Characters:

JACOB and **CALEB** (*brothers*)

VERA and **MIGUEL** (*friends of* **JACOB** and **CALEB**)

MR. LIM (*teacher*) **OFFICER DAVIES** (*police officer*)

Scene 1

Scene: *The classroom*

It's lunchtime. **MR. LIM** *is sitting at his desk. He's looking at an open folder.* **JACOB**, **VERA**, *and* **MIGUEL** *enter.* **MR. LIM** *doesn't look up.*

JACOB: Good afternoon, Mr. Lim!

MR. LIM: (*jumps up, closes the folder, and hides it behind his back*) Oh … hello, kids. I … didn't hear you come in.

VERA: Sorry to bother you, Mr. Lim.

MR. LIM: (*clearing his throat*) What can I do for you?

MIGUEL: It's about the science project. I can't find a partner.

JACOB: We thought Miguel could work with Vera and me. Is that okay?

MR. LIM: Three people does seem **reasonable** and fair. What is your project?

VERA: (*excitedly*) We're going to store popcorn kernels at different temperatures. Then we'll see if that affects, or changes, how well they pop.

MIGUEL: (*grinning*) And when we're done, we can eat the popcorn!

frozen

cold

room temperature

warm

3

MR. LIM: Is there anything else?

JACOB: No, that's all.

VERA: (*looking* concerned, *or worried, and trying to see behind* **MR. LIM's** *back*) Are you okay, Mr. Lim?

MR. LIM: (*moving so that* **VERA** *cannot see the folder*) I'm fine, Vera. It's just not the best time. I have a lot on my mind.

MIGUEL: Come on, Vera. Let Mr. Lim finish his lunch.

VERA: Oh, sure. Good-bye, Mr. Lim.

VERA *takes one more look at* **MR. LIM,** *then* **VERA, MIGUEL,** *and* **JACOB** *exit.*

Scene 2

Scene: *The school playground at lunchtime*

CALEB *finds* **JACOB**, **MIGUEL**, *and* **VERA**. **CALEB** *has a mitt on his hand and is carrying a baseball.*

CALEB: Hey, guys. What's up?

MIGUEL: We've just been talking about our science project with Mr. Lim.

VERA: And, boy, was he acting weird!

CALEB: What do you mean?

VERA: Well, for one thing, he couldn't wait for us to leave.

JACOB: Plus, he was hiding a folder.

CALEB: What folder?

VERA: He was looking at a folder when we came in. But when he saw us, he quickly **concealed** it behind his back.

CALEB: That's weird.

MIGUEL: He seemed upset too.

JACOB *and* **VERA** *nod.*

CALEB: Upset?

MIGUEL: Angry, would be more **precise**.

VERA: (*shaking her head*) He wasn't angry. I think he was worried. Maybe he received bad news from his family in South Korea.

JACOB: (*excitedly*) Or … maybe he's a spy! He was probably looking at top-secret papers!

CALEB: (*laughing*) A spy? I don't think so! Let's **reconsider** the facts. One, he's a teacher. Two, he hid a folder from you. He was just grading tests. Case solved!

JACOB: (*looking **stubborn***) I'm not giving up. It's more than that. Mr. Lim has something to hide.

CALEB: Okay, let's follow him after school. We'll see if he does anything **suspicious**.

MIGUEL: Good plan. Now, let's play ball!

MIGUEL *leads the others offstage.*

STOP AND CHECK

Why do the students think that Mr. Lim has a problem?

Scene 1

Scene: *The sidewalk outside school*

MR. LIM *is walking.* **VERA**, **MIGUEL**, **JACOB**, *and* **CALEB** *are following him.* **OFFICER DAVIES** *enters and starts talking with* **MR. LIM**. *The children are too far away to hear their conversation.*

VERA: What are they talking about?

MIGUEL: I'm not sure, but Mr. Lim doesn't look happy.

CALEB: That doesn't make sense. Officer Davies is Mr. Lim's friend.

JACOB: Maybe Mr. Lim is in trouble.

VERA: Look out—they're coming!

The children hide behind a bush. **MR. LIM** *and* **OFFICER DAVIES** *stop next to the bush.*

OFFICER DAVIES: I'd like you to come down to the police station tomorrow.

MR. LIM: I can't do that.

OFFICER DAVIES: (*pauses to think*) Then you'll have to come with me now.

MR. LIM: (*nodding*) Yes, I guess you're right.

MR. LIM *follows* **OFFICER DAVIES** *offstage.*

MIGUEL: (*standing up*) What was that about? (*The others stand up, too.*)

CALEB: (*shaking his head in* **confusion**) I don't understand what is happening, but I sure want to find out.

JACOB: Let's follow them!

JACOB *leads the way offstage.*

9

Scene 2

Scene: *Outside the local police station*

JACOB *and* **CALEB** *sit on a bench.* **VERA** *and* **MIGUEL** *stand next to them.*

JACOB: (*excitedly*) I told you Mr. Lim is a spy! He's giving information to the police right now!

VERA: (*shaking her head*) No, he got bad news from his family in Korea. He's asking the police for help.

MIGUEL: I think Mr. Lim is just paying some parking tickets. That's why he was upset at lunch.

CALEB: (*laughing*) I'm **astounded** at you three! You have too much imagination! Mr. Lim and Officer Davies are friends. Mr. Lim can't see him tomorrow, so he came today. Case closed!

JACOB: (*pointing offstage*) Maybe we should ask Mr. Lim. Here he comes now.

MR. LIM *enters. He sees the group and looks* **flustered** *and embarrassed.*

MR. LIM: Oh! … What are you doing here?

VERA: Is everything okay, Mr. Lim?

MR. LIM: I'm just a little **perplexed**. I'm very surprised to see you here.

MIGUEL: Mr. Lim, is there something going on? You can tell us.

MR. LIM: (*in a sharp tone*) You'll find out soon. I have to go now.

MR. LIM *exits.*

CALEB: (*surprised*) Mr. Lim never gets angry like that. How should we **interpret** this?

JACOB: It's the stress or worry from having a secret **identity**. Spies don't like people to find out who they really are.

> **STOP AND CHECK**
>
> Why are the children following Mr. Lim?

Act 3
MYSTERY SOLVED!

———— Scene 1 ————

Scene: *The next day in class*

MR. LIM *stands at the front of the class. He is yawning.* **JACOB**, **VERA**, *and* **MIGUEL** *sit at their desks chatting.*

VERA: Mr. Lim looks like he didn't sleep well. He must be worried about his family.

MIGUEL: No, he's worried about paying his parking tickets.

JACOB: Wrong! His cover has been blown. It's the worst thing that can happen to a spy.

MR. LIM: May I have everyone's **attention**, please? Listen, I have some important news.

Everyone stops talking.

VERA: (*whispering*) This is it! Pay attention.

MR. LIM: (*looking at* **VERA, MIGUEL,** *and* **JACOB**) As our more **inquisitive** class members know, I went to the police station yesterday. I didn't want to tell anyone why until I knew for sure. Then last night, I got the okay for a field trip to the old town jail.

MIGUEL: (*shocked*) The old town jail? But that's closed. No one is **allowed** to go there without special permission.

MR. LIM: (*smiling*) That's right. But my friend Officer Davies organized it for us. We're going to have a full tour!

The children start chatting excitedly.

VERA: Everything makes sense now. We all got it wrong.

JACOB: I still think he's a spy.

MIGUEL *rolls his eyes.*

MR. LIM: (*holding his hands up for quiet*) We'll get a real feel for our town's past.

MIGUEL: (*raising his hand*) When are we going?

MR. LIM: Next week. I was up late last night doing the paperwork. (*handing out papers*) Take these permission slips home and have them signed.

VERA: I can't wait to tell my mom!

JACOB: (*grinning*) I can't wait to tell Caleb. Case closed!

STOP AND CHECK

Why had Mr. Lim been acting so strangely?

Respond to Reading

Summarize

Summarize what happened and what each character thought in *The Mysterious Teacher*. Your graphic organizer may help you.

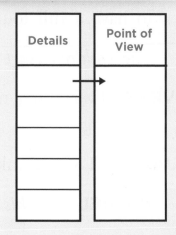

Details	Point of View

Text Evidence

1. In Act 1, Scene 2, what is Caleb's point of view about Mr. Lim? What does he say that shows this point of view? POINT OF VIEW

2. Look at the word *stress* on page 12. What clues help you know what *stress* means? VOCABULARY

3. Write about Mr. Lim's point of view. How does planning a surprise affect how he speaks and acts? Include examples from the dialogue and stage directions.
   WRITE ABOUT READING

Compare Texts

Read about a family that looks twice
to find an answer.

The Case of the Missing Nectarine

"Hey! There's a nectarine missing," cried Dad. He was preparing lunches for everyone. "I just bought them yesterday, and I told everyone they were for lunch today. So who took one?"

Mom peered over the newspaper. "I do love nectarines, but it wasn't me."

"Don't look at me, Dad. I haven't been in the kitchen," said Sarah.

"I know I bought four, one for each of us. So why are there are only three now?" asked Dad.

"Well, Sarah and I didn't eat it," answered Mom. "How about you, Josh?"

Josh looked up from his detective story. "Not guilty," he said.

Dad frowned and crossed his arms. "Somebody took it. Be honest."

Josh put down his book and jumped up. "Don't panic, Dad. I've read loads of detective books. I know just what to do."

Sarah rolled her eyes.

Josh ignored her. "First, we need to make sure there really is a crime to investigate. Where is the store receipt?"

Dad handed Josh the receipt from his wallet. Josh carefully weighed the nectarines on the kitchen scale. Then he checked the weight on the receipt.

"You're correct, Dad," Josh said. "One is missing."

Josh emptied the fruit bowl, and he looked in the fridge. There was no sign of the missing nectarine.

Next, Josh asked everyone the same question. "Where were you when Dad came home with the groceries yesterday?"

Mom and Sarah reminded Josh that they had been at swim practice. They couldn't have taken it.

Then Josh remembered something. "Dad, I saw you eating something when you were putting the groceries away!"

Dad looked embarrassed. "It wasn't a nectarine, Josh," he mumbled. "It was the last piece of Mom's chocolate cake. I couldn't resist it."

"Hmmm, this case is tough," said Josh. "We need to retrace your steps, Dad. First, pick up the shopping bag. Now show us exactly what you did."

Dad felt silly, but he reached for the bag. That was when Josh noticed the bulge at the bottom. "Case solved!" he cried. "The nectarine is still in the bag. Am I a great detective, or what?"

For once, Sarah did not say a word.

Make Connections

What did Josh do to solve the mystery in *The Case of the Missing Nectarine?* ESSENTIAL QUESTION

How did the characters in each of the stories find out the truth about the mysteries? TEXT TO TEXT

Focus on
Literary Elements

Foreshadowing In mystery stories or dramas, writers often give hints about what will happen later in the story. This is called foreshadowing. The author gives the reader clues before an event happens.

Read and Find Turn to page 2. Look for the clue. What is the author foreshadowing?

Your Turn

With a group, read Act 2, Scene 2 of *The Mysterious Teacher* aloud. Some people might need to read two parts. Read Mr. Lim's lines in a way that makes it clear to the audience that his behavior is very strange. Then talk about what event these clues foreshadow.